The Promised Child

Black, Bipolar and Baptized

Written by: Justina L. Mack

Thanks

First of all, I would like to give thanks to my Heavenly

Father, for without him, I am nothing. I couldn't have made it

Through this ordeal without such a powerful and deep

entervention.

He has inspired me to sit down and share these words

With someone who may be in desperation and feel like

There is no end to what some people call mania, but I call

it MADNESS.

I would like to thank my family. Especially, my mother,

Who when, I told her I was writing a book, she encouraged me all of the way. I would also like to thank, my sister Lisa, for

Without her, I would not be here today to even write this book.

I would be dead. She was the one that suggested that I get

Professional help in the first place and took me to every

hospital that there was, no matter, how far it was. She would

Always say I am not big on saying the words "I love you", but

"I will take you from here to Tibablue Missisippi to get you the

proper help". That is why I love her so much.

Table of Contents

Chapter 1. Growing Up In The Church

As early as I could remember, I always went to church.

My family started out as Pentecostal. Which for the one's who

don't know what that is. It is considered the holiness Church.

Laying on of hands, Speaking of Tongues, and being baptized

were all part of this Church. Oh, by the way, please don't let

me forget, casting out Demons.

There were times we were in Church from 6p.m. until

midnight.   I don't regret a day of it .

I am blessed to have been instilled with those values

Of Christianity at such a young age because I was never

Aware of what I was about to face in my later years in life.

I had my Lord and Savior to fall back on. Amen.

Chapter 2. The Promised Child

Let me start out by telling you a little bit about myself.

My name is Justina L. Mack. I am an African-American Female.

I was born in Oyster, Virginia, however, I was raised in a very

Small and narrowed-minded town called Palatka, Fl. It is

Located on the outside of Jacksonville,Fl.

For the most part, when I was growing up, life was good.

I grew up with plenty of neighborhood friends. Stick ball,

Dodge Ball, Tag, you name it we played it. Well, that was until

The street lights came on and then everybody had to go home.

In those days, we fought just like other kids, but we didn't

Kill. We fought fair.

I have a family of two brothers and three sisters. I guess

You could say I am the Middle child. Just in case if you haven't

Heard, let me tell you real quick. It has been said that middle

Children are always longing for attention.

Perhaps, but most of the time I thought I was just

misunderstood.

I did all kinds of things, starting when I was young to keep all eyes on me.

I was an A student, since the
first grade all the way

through College.

I took Piano lessons, even
though I hated them just so

I could be different and stand out.
My parents, were so proud,

They even went out and brought a
piano that they couldn't

Even afford.

Not to brag on myself, but I was
blessed with a beautiful

Singing voice, so I joined the glee
Club at School, so that I

could still have that constant
attention on me.

I think the craziest thing I did
was join the girls Basketball

team, knowing goodness well, I
hated to sweat.

I had so much potential, so
much promise, so much hope.

I had my life planned out. I was
going to attend an all black

University, and pledge to one of my favorite Sororities, and

graduate Suma-Cum-Laude. Then Later attend Grad-School

And become either a top Surgeon or one of the finest legal

professionals in town.

I was even saving my Virginity for my Husband.

We would have a boy for him and a girl for me and a house

On the Hills and eat Caviar and drink Champagne all day.

At least, this is how it was supposed to be……….

A life full of Promise…..

Chapter 3. The Darkness

In came the Darkness, after my first year in Junior College

Which is not the place I wanted to be in the first place, but

Because of finances and other things I had to sit home for a

year.

Needless to say, after being
home and feeling lonely, I

Met this young man, who will remain
nameless, however, I

Feel in love.   I was the first time I
had experienced anything

Like this and I didn't know what to do
with it . I just knew

That every time he came around I
felt funny.

After about, the end of that year, he talked me into

my first sexual experience. It was awefull . I knew I was saving

myself for my Husband and when I finished in came a huge

amount of guilt and shame and a feeling of dirtiness.

I felt as if all of my hopes and dreams were going to go up

in smoke. Little did I know what was about to happen.

Days later, I began to obsess about the idea of being

pregnant. I took over 10 home pregnancy tests. They all

came out negative. Weeks later, I went to see about two or

Three Gynecologist and the results were negative.   But, I

Was still obsessing, because in my mind, I disobeyed God

And I was supposed to be punished.

Along with the obsessing, came the lack of sleep,

And the feelings of despair, darkness, and last, but not

least Depression and Darkness.

       I started out feeling useless and that no good

could come of me. I couldn't concentrate, not even

to put a sentence together. I was afraid. Why was

This happening to me. Was I being cursed?

Finally, I just confided in my mom and told her what was

Going on with me and she understood, because she had

gotten pregnant with my brother at the age of 17.

She asked me if I had taken a test or gone to a doctor to

Actually find out if I was or not and I told her that the results

Were negative, but I can't seem to dig myself out of this dark

hole I was in.

It was then that my Mother and my Grandmother joined

Hands with me and told me to pray.
My Grandmother was con-

sidered a Prayer Warrior. They laid
hands on me and were

determined to rebuke that Demon
right out of me. Things like

Depression were not hear by African-
Americans in those days

And were felt like they were
Demonic forces that had to be

To be rebuked by God.

Chapter 4. Years of Clinics and
Hospitals

After months of praying and
rebuking spirits nothing

good was happening. I was only
getting worse. I had dropped

Out of College, because I couldn't
concentrate and then I

started having crying spells. I was just sad all of the time.

Later, my oldest sister Lisa, suggested to my mom and dad

That maybe I need some professional help.

It was then,I was taken to a small hospital where they gave me

An Antidepressant called Prozac. I
hated it. It made me feel

like I could feel the air leaving the top
of my head. So, I quit

taking it.

   After, stopping with the Prozac,
I ended up in a Manic

state. I was all over the place. I was
delusional, hyperactive,

and combative. You name it and I
was it.

I remember, I dressed and went
to a Lexus dealership

With no money and no income and
said that I was a famous

Recording artist with Motown
records and I wanted a car off

of the showroom floor.

It was then, I was taken to this famous Hospital by the

Name of Charter Springs in Ocala,Fl. And was diagnosed as

bipolar.   At that time, I was put on Lithium and some other

Drugs, but I liked the feeling of being able to have such a

High at times without the use of
drugs, I would stop taking

My meds on purpose or sometimes,
my meds had to be

adjusted.

In those Hospitals, they will
strap you down to the bed

And inject you with all types of medication to calm you down.

From the age of 19 to 33 I must have been hospitalized

at least 200 times.

Chapter 5. Stigma and Shame

In a small town, where I am from, people talk. They

Look, talk, and whisper, and talk some more.

They used say things like "she is smart, but she is as crazy,

as a bedbug." Furthermore, If they don't know something

About you, they will make up the rest. Just to make it sound

more juicier and interesting.

Because in that town, BLACK FOLK, DON 'T HAVE NO

MIND PROBLEMS!

They have drinking , drug, and gambling problems only.

Chapter 6. Rainbow

I was never a drinker, or a drug addict, and I used caution

playing the lottery.

However, the day I got pregnant, years later, in my late

30's was the best day of my life. My Psychiatrist at the time,

told me to abort the baby. He said
that the pregnancy would

Be just too risky. I could not afford
to be off of my meds that

Long to have a child and that it would
not be healthy.

I heard a voice from God which
told me that this Child was

going to be my healing.

I had to come off of all my medications at that time.

My meds were Depakote, Haldol, Seroquel, and so much more.

I did this just so the baby would be healthy, putting my own

life at risk.

Just as the Doctor had said came the Mania, I was all over

the place and pregnant. My family was worried, but I

Knew, even in my manic stage this child was from the Lord.

After being sent to about six or seven different Hospitals,

While pregnant and me refusing to take any medication that

would harm my child.

I was sent to a Hospital in Gainesville, FL., by the name of

Shands Teaching Hospital. They suggested that I receive ECT

treatments. Those are shocks of convulsive electrical magnetic

Waves to the brain to stimulated the depressed mood

behavior.   Low and Behold it
worked. After about 4 sessions, I

was healed. I suffered some memory
loss, but the baby was

fine and so was I.

Chapter 7. Sunsunshine

Now, that was 12 years ago and I have a healthy straight A

11 year old student, son. Who loves God first, and loves me

also.

Nothing is impossible, if you have faith in your Father,

Who is in Heaven, who can do all things, but fail you.

Lord, thank you, for the Sunshine at the end of the Rainbow.

www.ingramcontent.com/pod-product-compliance
Lightning Source LLC
Chambersburg PA
CBHW050843290526
45792CB00001B/498